WEYK GLOBAL
BOOK SERIES

ZACHARY LUKASIEWICZ

WEYK GLOBAL MEDIA
Lincoln, Nebraska
www.weykglobal.com

Related Courses & Workshops: WeykGlobal.com
LinkedIn: linkedin.com/in/zdrake2013
More about the author: weykglobal.com/leadership
Please send errors, comments, and speaking inquiries to
hey@weykglobal.com

The goal in releasing this book series is to help narrow the gap between professional marketers and industry newcomers. The idea here is to provide necessary information to passionate individuals to make their business dreams a reality. Our marketing materials - including our courses and workshops - are all aligned on this front.

For Whom Is This Book Intended?

This book is meant for start-ups and small businesses that lack marketing-savvy staff but have a need to intelligently expand the reach of their goods or services. These companies may not have the budget to hire external marketing help, and may also find traditional Google tools to be intimidating. We seek to educate and demystify the online marketplace for these organizations.

What Does It Do?

Using a series of lessons, case studies, and quizzes (if you opt for our online courses), this book and its entire series guides you through 3-5 minute story-based chapters on search marketing, content marketing, PR & Media and more. All in all, we cover eighteen different topics. Depending on your sense of humor, our case studies can cause a few chuckles as you think about, for example, how Connor the karaoke rental equipment guy should improve his search results.

The lessons in this book are heavy on strategy and light on execution. Though this book helps readers differentiate between marketing tactics and identify the best strategies for different businesses, it does not go so far as to provide a detailed walk-through of execution using Google tools. That said, it certainly provides enough information to begin taking steps in the right direction.

How Does It Do It?

This book handles dry topics well, making consistency paramount. This keeps readers engaged in the lessons, with no time to lose focus.

Not only highly interactive, the chapters are also very brief at 3-5 minutes. There are also notes about various courses and workshops to help reinforce the takeaways.

Recommending This Book

Reviewing all of the chapters takes less than 45 minutes. As a digital marketing instructor for Growth(X) Academy, I integrate these essentials into my lessons on search marketing and content marketing in order to reinforce concepts.

FIND YOUR CUSTOMERS WITH CUSTOMER LIFETIME VALUE

- Are all customers created equal?
- What exactly is customer lifetime value?
- How can I use it to help my business?

It goes without saying that customers are good. Without them, your business would be...well, not a business. But does that mean they all have equal value?

Imagine there's a business called Yasui Yo-Yos. Their handcrafted yo-yos are popular with a variety of customers, but they want to focus on attracting and retaining the "right" ones.

Yasui Yo-Yos sorts their current customers into different types and starts evaluating each for their long-term business value.

While we hypothesized which Yasui Yo-Yos customers would be the most valuable, there's a better way to do this: customer lifetime value (CLV).

CLV is your chance to be all "Me Me Me." Instead of just looking at your customers' likes, wants, and needs, you can say, "What about my needs? How valuable are these customers to me? How much of my money should I spend to get them?"

CLV helps you answer those questions by looking at the entire relationship you have with a type of customer and estimating how much that person is worth to your business.

Knowing your target buyers' CLV helps you grow your base of "right" customers, which helps you decide how much you're willing to spend to keep those customers coming back.

LISTEN UP
So how do you figure out your customers' CLV? Math.

It can get tricky and there's different ways to do it. But to help you get your feet ever-so-gently wet, we'll show you one of the simplest ways to do CLV math.

Let's say Harry owns a hotel called Harry's Home Away from Home. To get his CLV, he needs to research how his business has performed in the past.

The 3 "past behaviors" he should look at are the average annual transactions per customer, average profit per transaction, and average number of years people remain customers.

For average annual transactions per customer, he notes that most of his guests visit once a year.

To get the average profit per transaction, he looks at the average final guest bill, which is $1000 per person. After subtracting expenses like housekeeping, Harry estimates he makes a 25% profit off each bill – so that's $250 profit per customer.

For the average number of years customers remain, he calculates that his guests normally return at least once in the following year, meaning they stay on as customers for 2 years.

Harry takes the numbers (1 stay per year, $250 profit per customer, visiting 2 years in a row) and plugs them into a formula.

Here's the formula: (Average Annual Transactions Per Customer) x (Average Profit Per Transaction) x (Average # of Years Customers

Remain) = CLV

And here's how it looks with Harry's info plugged in: (1) x ($250) x (2) = $500 CLV

Now that Harry knows his CLV is $500, he can try and improve it by keeping his current customers around longer, or use it to help him target and convert valuable potential customers.

Let's see how Harry might get his customers to stick around longer.

After checking things out, Harry realizes that giving customers more personalized attention will encourage them to return several times over the following years. He brainstorms a few ways he can do this.

When his clients have upcoming birthdays, he'll send them an offer for a "Happy Home Away from Home Birthday" package that has discounts on luxury suites and hotel amenities.

He'll also create a loyalty program that gives customers 25% off hotel stays when they make it past that crucial 2-year mark and come back to his hotel for a third year.

Now let's check out how Harry can use CLV to help him convert potential customers.

Harry realizes he can use his $500 CLV to evaluate which of his marketing efforts are the most effective at bringing in new customers.

Right now, he has his advertising budget split equally between these 3 channels: billboards near the airport, mobile ads targeted at vacationing families, and search engine marketing targeted at business travelers.

To find out which is working better for him, Harry calculates each advertising channel's CLV.

He starts by grouping his current customers by the channel they found his hotel through. Using his trusty formula, he then calculates the CLV of each customer group – which then becomes that marketing channel's CLV.

His billboards have a $325 CLV and the mobile ads a $480 CLV. But the search ads have a $750 CLV, which is higher than his overall CLV of $500. He should consider putting more of his ad budget into search ads targeting business travelers.

Harry's CLV calculations also helped him figure out the most valuable potential customers for his hotel: business travelers.

When he calculated his business traveler customers' CLV, he discovered that they usually stayed at his hotel more often than once a year, so they had a higher average number of annual transactions than other guests.

He also found out that they remained customers longer than the 2-year average of other guests and that they spent more than vacationing families.

So Harry should do more than just up his search ads budget. He should consider spending more on marketing to business travelers in general.

DO THIS NOW
Let's do a guesstimate of a CLV for your business. No pressure...it's okay to take a stab at your average transactions or other numbers.

If you're participating in the course, go to the next section to access your self assessment.

KEY TAKEAWAYS
1. Certain customers can be more valuable to your business than others.
2. CLV uses past behavior (and math) to estimate how valuable customers are to your business.
3. It helps you refine the amount of ad budget you're giving

to each of you're marketing channels.

HOW CROWDFUNDING SUCCESS BEGINS WITH AN EMAIL

- Why do I need to market my crowdfunding campaign?
- How can I use email marketing to attract potential backers?
- How do I plan an effective email marketing campaign?

Let's say you have a crowdfunding campaign all set up and ready to go. How do you get the word out?

It's not as easy as you might think. Crowdfunding sites host thousands of campaigns that are all competing for potential backers. Even if you have a great idea or product, getting noticed takes a lot of work.

Wait, isn't attracting backers why you put a project on a crowdfunding site in the first place? Yes, but the truth is that in today's world, even Edison's "light bulb" idea would benefit from a smart marketing plan.

There are a lot of marketing strategies, channels, and platforms to choose from.

Which is the most effective strategy to attract potential backers to your crowdfunding campaign?Crowdfunding isn't just about building brand awareness or gathering followers, it's about gaining momentum and attracting potential backers quickly.

Campaigns that raise 30% to 50% or more of their goal in the first

48 hours raise 47% more money on average on Indiegogo. That means that all of your pre-launch planning should focus on your launch day.

With a limited time frame to reach your goal, using broader outreach tactics simply isn't efficient. That's why email works: It's an active form of communication that lets you speak directly to your target audience.

On average, people engage with an email longer than a tweet or a post because it's considered a more serious form of communication. This gives you the time to explain the idea in detail, and how backing it will benefit them.

But how do you find people to contact? The best email lists consist of customers that you have developed a relationship with over time.

First, email your closest contacts, which includes family and friends. Send them a personalized message with a specific call to action, or CTA, that will lead them to your campaign page.

Next, message larger contact groups, like co-workers and business associates. Once you've established support from those 2 groups, message peripheral contacts, like your college's alumni email list.

You can build your email list by going to or hosting events. Connecting with communities is the first step for most successful campaigns.

Use your social presence: Create a CTA on your personal and social channels that encourages potential backers to sign up for your emails and get in on the action early.

Ready to send? Wait a second. People get several emails a day soliciting everything from TVs to travel, and many remain unopened or in the spam folder.

The hardest part about email marketing is getting people to actually open the emails. So before you get into thinking about the email's content, you'll need to come up with an effective email subject line.

A good email subject line is to-the-point, but also hints at the story behind your idea. There isn't one way to come up with one, but here a few pointers: Don't be generic, make it feel personal, and create a sense of urgency.

The official email campaign should start a week before the launch, and every piece of communication should work to build momentum and create anticipation.

One week before launch: Send an email reminding your audience about the upcoming campaign, and that they're eligible for a secret deal or special pricing.

3 days before launch: Send another email sharing the specifics of the deal and letting your backers know the exact time of launch.

Launch day: Send an email when you launch letting people know it's go time. A good launch email has a strong CTA and a high-res photo that gets people excited about the project.

These early emails aren't only good for creating anticipation. By offering different price points pre- launch, you can gauge people's reactions and get a real market estimation of your product's value.

TOOLS
If you have a big email list, use an email platform like Mailchimp or Constant Contact. This will allow you to send a variety of emails and increase your email open rates.

The first days of a crowdfunding campaign are crucial to its success. This is the time to build on the momentum you created in the pre-launch phase.

During the second week after launch, email everyone who hasn't contributed yet and offer them one final deal. Remind them that even if they can't contribute, they can offer support by spreading the word to their friends.

During the campaign you can have flash sales, boost efforts on social media, and create messaging with a "last chance" offer.

Once the crowdfunding campaign has finished and the product has launched in market, raise the price so that your backers feel like they got a special deal. Most importantly, send an email thanking them, because they are your future clientele.

DO THIS NOW
Now that you've learned how to create an email marketing plan for a crowdfunding campaign, let's create a sample email subject line for your campaign.

If you're participating in the course, go to the next section to access your self assessment.

KEY TAKEAWAYS
1. Email marketing is a good way to speak directly to potential backers.
2. Special offers and early bird perks are a great incentive for backers to take action and contribute.
3. Having an email subject line that's unique and creates a sense of urgency will increase your email open rates.

INNOVATIVE CROWDFUNDING: RAISE MORE THAN MONEY

- Why should I consider crowdfunding?
- How can I use crowdfunding to connect with my target audience better?
- How do I use it to test out new products or ideas?

Say "crowdfunding" and people usually think of a lean startup seeking funds or an idealistic firebrand raising money for a cause.

It's easy to imagine them creating a prototype of their idea, filming a cool promo video, posting them on a crowdfunding site, raising a ton of money, and BAM — finding huge success.

When you put aside these stereotypes, though, you can begin to see how crowdfunding can be a valuable tool for brands of all sizes.

Done well, crowdfunding can help you create stronger connections with your target audience.

In social media marketing, people engage by clicking, liking, and sharing. With crowdfunding, they're offering something much more valuable: money. And that's a huge vote of confidence for your brand.

This type of monetary engagement can make your audience feel less like a customer and more like a stakeholder in the success of your product or project.

Imagine there's a brand of healthy snacks called Benny's Bran Bites. They not only believe in healthy eating, but an overall healthy lifestyle.

Benny's decides to expand beyond their Bran Bite business and launch a research and discovery lab that will explore new, innovative ideas or products that will help society live healthier.

They use a crowdfunding campaign to help spread the word about their lab as well as gain support for it. They start by asking college students to submit their ideas about what project the lab should tackle first.

Benny's chooses the best 5 submissions and asks each of these finalists to create their own page on a crowdfunding website. The competitors are then given a set amount of time to gain support and raise funds for their ideas.

A winner is chosen based on the quality of their idea and how much funding they raised. They get an internship in Benny's lab, working with experts to bring their idea to life. Benny's also gives the other finalists $10,000 in funding.

This crowdfunding campaign not only gives Benny's lab its starter project, but helps anyone who's pledged money to the winner or the finalists feel like they invested in the lab.

To do a crowdfunding campaign, you should have a general idea of your mission and donation goal. But more importantly, you need a good idea.

Whether it's an innovative concept or an upcoming product, you can test the market and get feedback from the public.

Crowdfunding campaigns give you the luxury of a large-scale

audience telling you if your idea or product is popular enough to launch. If you don't get a resounding "heck yes, we'd buy this" from them, you may decide not to pursue the idea.

You can also find out what features people would like to see improved or removed entirely. You might even discover a great potential feature you hadn't considered yet.

Let's say Benny's first lab project is a miniature food sensor that scans meals for nutritional content. They decide to test this product while it's still in development.

Benny's creates another crowdfunding campaign. This time, their goal is to get feedback and insights from a large community which will help them improve the food sensor's design.

They offer a test version of their food sensor as a perk to anyone contributing to their campaign. The community shows a lot of interest in it, but Benny's also receives comments asking why the sensor isn't offered as a wearable device.

Based on this feedback, Benny's redesigns the food sensor into an accessory that easily clips onto a watch, a bracelet, a belt, or a keychain.

Better yet, Benny's crowdfunding campaign generates more than just valuable insights. They also get a lot of buzz and excitement around their food sensor – AKA, free PR.

DO THIS NOW
To come up with your own crowdfunding campaign, you should first hone in on a business goal or need.

If you're participating in the course, go to the next section to access your self assessment.

KEY TAKEAWAYS
1. Crowdfunding can help brands engage customers, test ideas, and increase exposure.

2. When people fund a brand's project or idea, it helps them feel like stakeholders versus just customers.
3. Brands can use crowdfunding to get feedback on new and/or innovative product or ideas.

BUILD YOUR BUSINESS FAST WITH GROWTH HACKING

- What's growth hacking?
- How is it different from traditional marketing?
- How can I find my growth hack?

Even if you're new to growth hacking, you probably already have a hunch about what it is. Or more specifically, what it does.

Growth hacking is all about – you guessed it – growth. It's a marketing style where every tactic is geared toward rapidly building a business.

You've probably seen a growth hack (or even been influenced by one) without knowing it. In fact, you may have used a growth hack in your own marketing without realizing you were doing it. Ready to see if you can spot one?

Growth hacking started as the love child between developers and marketers.

These were people who wanted to promote their startups quickly but didn't have a large advertising budget or any traditional training.

Today, it's something that can be used by anyone. Though it helps for you (or someone on your team) to have technical expertise, growth hacking is really about having the right mindset.

This isn't about a structured set of rules and steps. Instead, you need to think about growth all the time... preferably as soon as your business idea comes down from Idea Heaven.

That way, you can find low-cost loopholes that can help you get more customers – fast.
Let's check out which tactics growth hackers use and which ones traditional marketers rely on.

A lot of well-known companies used growth hacking back in their not-so-well-known days, and not all of them relied on heavy technical expertise.

For example, the creators of email organizer Mailbox App made a public waiting list for their product, which soon had over 1 million people on it.

And in 2012, online marketplace Etsy added "Pin It" buttons to its site so people could easily share Etsy items on Pinterest. This helped Etsy sellers promote their shops and Pinterest users realize each item was for sale.

The Etsy story shows how growth hacking isn't passive: You need to find and join the communities your customers are in. Let's take a closer look at how Etsy did this.

Etsy noticed that many of their members were active Pinterest users, and would pin items they found on Etsy to their Pinterest boards.

This inspired them to add the "Pin It" button, helping people share items on Pinterest with just one click. It also helped Etsy's sellers, as each pin or post would include the seller's name and a link to purchase the item on Etsy.

As more shoppers and sellers pinned items found on Etsy, the marketplace became a top source of pins on Pinterest – which introduced new people to Etsy every day.

Etsy encouraged the Pinterest cross-pollination further by giving their sellers tips and tricks on how they could use the social network to promote their shops and showcase their items for sale.

They also started a curated "Guest Pinner" series on their own Pinterest page, featuring sellers, influencers, and brands. This kept Etsy's audience engaged and raised interest in the platform.

DO THIS NOW
Growth hacking is all about finding opportunities to tell your customers about your business. Let's make a list of some of the growth hacks that might be right for you.

If you're participating in the course, go to the next section to access your self assessment.

KEY TAKEAWAYS
1. Growth hacking is a low cost alternative to traditional marketing.
2. It's a way of thinking that's focused on growing your customer base quickly.
3. There are different approaches to growth hacking - some are more technical, some are more creative.

TEST PRODUCT/ MARKET FIT BEFORE YOU COMMIT

- What's product/market fit?
- Why is it so important for my business?
- How do I go about finding it?

You know what the single worst marketing decision you can make is? Starting with a product nobody wants or needs.

For example, imagine there's a business called Nice-Ice. They make a product that turns fresh, falling snow into delicious, colorful slushies the whole family will enjoy.

Nice-Ice needs an environment where it snows often, so the company targets people living in colder climates.

But did Nice-Ice think about whether this audience really wanted snow slushies or not?

Product/market fit, or PMF, is being in a good market (big or profitable enough) with a proven and verified product that people in that market want and need.

It's hugely important. You can have the best team and the best product, but it doesn't matter if the market isn't there or your product doesn't properly meet the market's needs.

That means PMF is something you must nail early, as in before-you-spend-a-lot-of-money-and-build-your-product early.

But what if you've already built your product?

Well, it's pretty easy to tell if PMF is happening or not.

To get PMF, you need to come up with a business hypothesis, create a minimum viable product (MVP), and test the two against each other.

To come up with your business hypothesis, ask yourself: Who will use my product? What problems do they have? How can my product help solve their problems?

Next, create an MVP. It's your product in its simplest form. You can use it to help you test and prove your hypothesis to make sure you're solving people's problems (and attracting a good amount of interest).

To test your MVP, ask: Do people care about my product? Do they use it regularly? And see if you can track how they're using it so you'll know if what you're doing is right.

If your MVP doesn't support your hypothesis, you might have to pivot – AKA course-correct to test a new hypothesis or strategy. It's actually pretty common, so don't worry.

You might focus on a more compelling product feature, redesign for a new market, create a different hypothesis and solution, or find an entirely new idea. Regardless, it often means major product revisions or possibly starting over again.

For example, Airbnb wasn't always a community-driven hospitality company. It used to revolve around air mattresses on a living room floor.

Originally called airbedandbreakfast.com, Airbnb started during a popular design conference in San Francisco. The founders offered attendees their airbeds in their living room as well as breakfast.

They had some early success, but wanted a better PMF. So instead of focusing on just conferences, they pivoted to go after travelers who needed a place to stay anywhere in the world.

They began to bill their service as a way for travelers to find local, authentic accommodations and network at the same time. And, of course, get free breakfast every morning.

After listening to feedback, they became Airbnb and started helping anyone list or book any type of accommodation (castles, private islands, etc) in 34,000 cities around the world. And the rest is PMF history.

DO THIS NOW
Let's do the first step for finding PMF: Create your business hypothesis.

If you're participating in the course, go to the next section to access your self assessment.

KEY TAKEAWAYS
1. You should find PMF before you build your product and before you start marketing heavily.
2. To get it, create a hypothesis, build an MVP, and then start testing both.
3. Sometimes getting to PMF means you have to pivot or make sacrifices.

USE PROTOTYPING TO FAIL INTELLIGENTLY

- What's prototyping and why should I do it?
- What can I prototype?
- What are the different stages of prototyping?

When people hear the word "prototype," they normally think of robots, machines, or gadgets – usually with a lot of loose wires hanging off them.

But we want to talk about prototyping as an action. It's building and testing various "draft" versions of your idea – all designed to help you figure out that idea and develop it.

It could mean building one of those wired-up gadgets, or it could be as simple as drawing a sketch on paper.

But what kind of ideas or products can you prototype?

Think about it this way: Prototyping is about failing early so you don't fail late.

It's not about getting it right the first time, or even the second time. It's about rapidly improving your idea through trial and error, which is a lot less risky than blowing it out fully and then testing it.

But why even build a prototype? After all, it would be simpler to just ask people some questions in a survey. Here's the thing...you need to build something to really learn about it.

If you show an abstract idea to people, they're more likely to respond hypothetically. But prototyping gives them something tangible they can interact with and react to. This will get you better, more valuable feedback.

TIP

Make sure you're using your prototype to ask a question, not just show people your idea. Think about what you need to learn to keep improving and iterating.

Don't worry about things looking pretty. You'll get to the polishing stage after you get the info you need.

Now that you know the What and Why of prototyping, let's revisit that "you can prototype anything" claim. Seriously, you can.

Let's say you're a chef who's creating a new dish. Before you debut it in your restaurant, you could test and improve the recipe by creating different versions for people to try. You could then use their feedback to tweak and refine your dish.

A department store could prototype their sales experience by creating a replica of their retail store. There, they could test out ideas like a new store layout or an in-store mobile app before they launch them in their actual stores.

You could prototype how you work. One day a week could be your "prototype day," when you'd try things like having meetings only before 1pm or doing them all standing up. Whatever works, you'd add to your normal schedule.

The future of healthcare can even be prototyped. Kaiser Permanente uses the Garfield Innovation Center to do just that. It includes replicas of hospital rooms, doctor's offices, and people's houses. It even has robots.

Their prototyping involves cardboard mockups, technology simulations, and recreated workflows. This allows them to tweak processes and methods in a safe environment.

In all these examples, prototyping isn't a one-shot deal. It's about building, testing, tweaking, building, testing, tweaking, building, testing, tweaking...

... building, testing, tweaking, building, testing, tweaking, building, testing, tweaking... okay, okay, you get it. Let's look at the different types of prototypes you can do for different stages of your idea.

When you're in the early stages of developing your idea, you can prototype to explore it. This usually involves moving it from an abstract concept into a simple physical, digital, or experiential item.

Once you have a solid concept, you might not know how it would actually work. That's when you can prototype to learn how people's innate behavior can shape your product's behavior.

As you flesh out your idea, you may have specific questions about a certain feature or aspect. For example, should it be blue or red? What age group will it appeal to? You can prototype to test to get people's feedback.

Now let's match some scenarios to prototyping stages. Remember: You explore by creating a simple physical item early on. You learn when people's behavior tells you how your product should work. You test when you have specific questions about a feature.

The good news is you don't need a fully-baked concept to start prototyping.

Even if you only have the smallest wisp of an idea, you're ready to start prototyping. In fact, prototyping can help you think through your idea.

Your initial prototypes can be as simple as sketches. Just make sure to do at least 2 different versions so you can compare and contrast them.

DO THIS NOW

An easy way to try prototyping is to start with your work environment or schedule. For example, you could prototype how you do meetings, how your workspace looks, where you work, or your daily schedule.

If you're participating in the course, go to the next section to access your self assessment.

KEY TAKEAWAYS

1. Prototyping is about improving you're idea through trial and error.
2. Anything can be prototyped.
3. You can prototype to explore, learn, and test.

WEYK GLOBAL LEADERSHIP

Zachary Lukasiewicz is the Managing Director of Weyk Global.

Originally from Omaha, Nebraska and attended Drake University in Des Moines, Iowa. He served as a tri-chair for the Human Capital committee of Capital Crossroads, the 10-year plan for Central Iowa, where he focused on the attraction and retention of Des Moines residents from cradle to career.

Zachary has operated 50+ accelerator assistance programs and in-house workshops, and staffed marketing teams around the globe.

Zachary's focus is marketing investment - sourcing the best talent, recruiting domain experts and executing on his proven playbook and delivering the best possible experience. He sets the strategic direction and client profile within the program, including a curated team of mentors, investors and business advisors.

Zachary is responsible for making the initial relationships. He takes overall ownership of each programs' success and partners with other operations units external to Weyk Global to ensure exceptional delivery of exceptional marketing programs, and is ultimately responsible for turning good companies into great ones.

Additional:

• Builds systems around market research and data-driven management—especially in budget allocation, paid/organic, and navigating complex customer cadences.
• Experience building marketing infrastructure and communication processes throughout US Techstars classes, reducing acquisition costs with greater capacity and cost-effectiveness
• A recognized expert on US social media in real estate, education, and human resources industries
• A leader with proven skills working with innovative teams to build customer consensus and drive buy-in behavior across purpose-driven organizations
• Motivates large organizations and individual personnel to award-winning performance and achievement
• Leadership experience encompasses direct management of 20+ personnel, over $8.5 million in assets/budgets with a record of five enterprise acquisitions and assisting in seven fundraising rounds

Zachary has served as a management consultant with startups backed by White Star Capital, Hoxton Ventures, Bloomberg Beta, Real Ventures, BDC Capital, Chris Anderson. Eduardo Gentil, Jacqueline Novogratz, Mehdi Alhassani, Ana Carolina, Entrepreneur, Obvious Ventures, MIT, Ittleson Foundation, J.M.Kaplan Fund, SC/E, MassCEC, WhiteHouse.gov, ServiceCorps, The One Foundation, The Godley Family Foundation, the Boston Foundation, Boris Jabes, Ilya

Sukhar, Chris DeVore, Alex Payne, DJF, Liquid 2 Ventures, GSF, Sanjay Jain, Felix Anthony, Uma Raghavan, and TiE LaunchPad. Zachary's early experience comes from working under business leaders at market-leading companies including ISoft Data Systems, LukeUSA, AlphaPrep.net, Staffing Nerd, Immun.io, Reflect.io, Validated.co, Shaun White Enterprises, Solstice.us, Swym, Staffing Robot, Hatchlings, Coaching Actuaries, 8 to Great, Target, Paylease, MidAmerican Energy, and R&R Realty Group.

Weyk Global offers two types of in-house training:

- Our workshops at any location:

All advertised courses can be taught in the location of your choice at a time convenient for you. We will ensure the course is specific to your business and sector.

- Our workshops tailored to your needs:

We can design bespoke training to meet the needs of your business. You can provide a brief or we will work with you to develop the training resources to help you achieve your goals.

Analytics Fundamentals

Discover the fundamentals of analytics and the different tools that will help you draw insights from analytics.

In this workshop, we'll examine the fundamentals of analytics, exploring the tools and their most appropriate use. You'll discover how to draw insights from analytics, enabling you to predict emerging trends. This course is designed for those who are curious in nature, enjoy problem-solving and prefer a self- learning, exploratory approach to knowledge.

Career Accelerator

Ensure you have the skills and knowledge to quickly start making an impact in your organization.

Getting into the industry is always challenging; university provides many of the concepts but not necessarily all the skills to be really ready to make a difference. This workshop enables junior marketers to be successful sooner, by understanding the basic concepts and platforms of their day-to-day jobs and getting the skills they need to become more effective in their roles.

Content Marketing Strategy

Examine all areas of content marketing and the role they play in digital, marketing and business strategies.

Best-practice case studies will walk you through all the components of an effective content strategy. You'll also focus on how to create, distribute and manage your content.

Consumers prefer to be engages with a brand via a story or conversation, so the power of content is immeasurable. Through both in-class discussion and practical exercises, we'll explore how consumer behavior fuels this power and how you can develop your content marketing strategy to be just as powerful. You'll also learn how to properly measure its effectiveness.

Conversion Rate Optimization

Harness the power of conversion and learn how to optimize your site to achieve your online objectives.

This powerful workshop will teach you the fundamentals of how to turn your hard-earned website visitors into leads and sales. Applying the insights you'll get will help you improve your conversion rates leading to increased online revenue and lead generation. If you want to know more about the fast-growing marketing discipline of conversion rate optimization, this is the best workshop for you to dip your toe in the water and get started.

Copywriting (Advanced)

Explore new, clever and engaging ways to push your writing to the next level.

Writing today is an indispensable skill and if you want to excel, you need more than just the basics. Throughout this workshop, you'll engage with and produce strategic and compelling copy that will attract readers.

Copywriting (Essentials)

Discover the essential techniques for writing effective copy.

One of our most popular workshops, copywriting essentials explores the structure, rules and techniques in copywriting. Learn to craft compelling headlines, structure documents and most importantly, engage your reader.

Copywriting for Content Marketing

Plan, write and publish creative content that engages readers and keeps them coming back for more.

During this course, you'll explore copywriting for blogs, PR, social media posts and articles. Discover new techniques and master traditional ones. Explore a variety of effective, compelling and fresh techniques for copywriting for content marketing during this hands-on workshop.

Creative Leadership

Develop senior creative leadership skills to improve business effectiveness.

Winning the promotion and becoming a senior manager

doesn't mean you are ready for all that is ahead of you as you take on more responsibility and manage a team or sets of teams. Becoming a good leader in the new digital economy is not an easy task as there are many opportunities and challenges to tackle every single day. This course will help develop a creative culture, nurture creative talent, help build trusted business relationships that allow you and others to succeed and link business and creative needs with technology and innovation.

Customer Journey Mapping

Ensure customer understanding is at the heart of your marketing.

Create a compelling experience for customers using analytics tools and insights. Customer insights are a crucial part of any marketing strategy or campaign, and yet most marketing strategies are developed with a focus on the product attributes or benefits we want to communicate. In this course, you'll discover the fundamentals of analytics and the different tools that will help you draw insights from data to create a compelling customer experience.

CX for CMOs

This workshop brings together all the critical pieces you need to know in the age of information excess.

CX is not one thing, it's every way the customer experiences your brand and business. This workshop, curated by CMOs, brings together all of the critical pieces that are demanded of CMOs today in delivering customer experience - the holy grail of marketing – giving you real clarity on how to apply these insights to your business.

Data Analytics for Marketers

Engage with data analysis and discover how it can deliver

marketing effectiveness.

This short workshop will help you make sense of the high volume and increasingly complex data available to marketers, as well as build a high-level view of the tools, techniques and processes you might use in the process.

Data Driven Marketing Leadership

Broaden your skill set as a leader and develop a data-driven marketing mindset to support your technical team leaders.

During this workshop, you'll be provided with an outline of how business operations and governance work within the field of data, how to lead and inspire your technical teams and to provide cross-functional management and integration.

Data Driven Marketing Practitioner

Learn how to use data to drive your business forward.

In this workshop, we'll show you how to access both primary and third-party data, develop actionable insights, explore data research and perform analytical techniques. This will help you to tell stories with data, benchmark insights from analytics and incorporate the latest solutions and models to tackle business problems. Our Data-driven Practitioner Workshop is designed for those who have access to data directly and/or who have a team and prefer a self-learning, exploratory approach to learning.

Data Driven Marketing Strategy

Discover how a data-driven marketing strategy can deliver a successful customer-centric marketing presence.

In this workshop, we examine a more strategic approach to using your data. This allows us to uncover information about how customers interact with your brand and identify areas that would otherwise go undetected.

Data Visualization

Establish your own visualization techniques that will help sell your analytics results to business decision makers.

In this workshop, you'll learn how to translate and present analytics in an enticing manner. You'll draw upon insights from data and convert these into commercial insights. This workshop is designed for those who are curious in nature, enjoy problem-solving and prefer a self-learning, exploratory approach to knowledge.

Digital Analytics for Marketers

Introducing an accessible approach to measuring, analyzing and optimizing digital marketing activity.

Learn to apply proven marketing theories to real world examples. Unlock the power of data to enhance decision making and campaign planning. This workshop has been designed so a difficult topic is now simple, straightforward and easy to grasp.

Digital Copywriting Essentials

Discover the essential skills and practices for writing effective digital copy.

Whether it's a quick status update or detailed blog post, writing on a digital platform is already a part of your day. The structures and styles for online are, however, different - there is no one-size-fits-all approach to different platforms. For your copy to cut through the current cluttered digital environment, it needs to be engaging. Through tested techniques, you'll discover the art of writing engaging digital copy for search purposes, emails, websites and social media.

Digital Marketing Campaign Planning & Management

Broaden your skills base by discovering how digital can make your campaigns thrive.

During this workshop, you'll explore the practical elements of digital marketing and how you can integrate them within your brand's activity. You'll learn to determine the right resources, budget, plan and identify opportunities for optimization.

Digital Marketing Channels

Discover how each digital marketing channel can deliver you a customer-centric marketing presence.

In this workshop, we examine each channel individually and uncover information about channel contributions to the consumer journey and how to utilize it in your marketing activity.

Digital Marketing Essentials

Discover industry tips and tricks for successfully incorporating digital channels into your campaigns.

In this two-day intensive workshop, you'll explore the foundations of each digital channel, how they work and how they can fit together to deliver on your marketing objectives. We'll also look at digital tactics, strategies and processes and how you can tie them all together in an effective way.

Digital Marketing Foundations

Broaden your skill set and develop a foundational knowledge of the digital landscape, data, content and customer experience.

During this workshop you'll be provided with an outline of the core foundations and principles of digital marketing. Explore the role of data and content and how this can shape customer experience.

Digital Marketing Strategy

Uncover a framework for successful digital marketing.

Whether it's your business, industry, or campaign, digital continues to have a significant impact on the way we operate. During this workshop, you'll be provided with a framework for crafting a digital marketing strategy. To get the most out of this two-day intensive workshop, you should have a good understanding of the basic digital marketing tactics.

Email Marketing

Boost your email marketing results with proven techniques, technical and strategy improvements.

Explore new ways of using email marketing in your overall communications strategy and learn how to deploy marketing automation techniques to drive customer engagement.

Practical Predictive Analytics

Develop a deeper understanding of predictive analytics.

Using predictive analytics, discover how you can forecast, model and optimize data to create opportunities and prevent loss. To get the most out of this course, you should have a solid knowledge of analytics and have ideally spent some time working in the field - over three years' experience is recommended.

Privacy & Marketing Compliance

A commercial approach to compliance for data-driven marketers and advertisers.

Learn how to protect and enhance your brand's reputation by ensuring your marketing and advertising meets customer expectations and complies with the privacy and marketing content laws.

Programmatic Advertising

Adopt a simple, fresh and effective platform to power your marketing.

Programmatic advertising is reshaping the digital landscape as it's automating everything. Marketers need to exploit the power of automated media trading and learn how they can optimize its productivity. In this workshop, we'll explore various programmatic models and the different technologies available for implementation.

Retention & Loyalty Marketing Strategy

Discover the four pillars to building a comprehensive customer retention and loyalty marketing strategy.

In this two-day intensive workshop, you'll adopt a framework for retaining customers through loyalty marketing strategies. We'll explore the power behind loyalty and advocacy initiatives in both traditional and digital techniques. The proven effectiveness of keeping a customer and nurturing their loyalty and advocacy is where the value is derived.

SEM Essentials

Simple yet successful ways to enhance your search results.

Paid search can transform your business without a huge spend. It's a cost effective, highly convenient channel. See how it can strengthen your search engine marketing, morph into a wider digital strategy for your business and leverage other channels.

Sentiment Analysis

Discover best-practice approaches that use modern text mining and predictive analytics techniques to gain insight into consumer opinions and forecast behaviors.

In this course, you'll advance your knowledge of sentiment and content analysis, and opinion mining, develop a deeper understanding of how to work with unstructured text data (in particular, data retrieved from social media) and learn how traditional machine learning/predictive analytics techniques can be used for the purposes of sentiment analysis. It is recommended that you complete the Practical Predictive Analytics Workshop prior to taking this workshop. This workshop is designed for those who are curious in nature, enjoy problem solving and prefer a self-learning, exploratory approach to knowledge.

SEO Essentials

Find out how SEO drives new customers and better customer engagement.

Score page rankings, better click-throughs, utilize research tools and foster great external links with an effective SEO strategy. Discover what simple techniques can do when applied to your website structure.

Social Media Marketing Essentials

Discover the foundations behind social media marketing and how you can adopt the practices into your own communications mix.

Get up to speed with the latest trends, techniques and technologies in social media and learn to craft your own social media campaign through planning, execution and optimization.

Social Media Marketing Strategy

Research, plan and implement a successful social media marketing strategy from the ground up.

Most organizations and brands are on social media - and if they're not, they should be. Social media is a way for consumers to engage and communicate with brands. But this doesn't mean businesses should just start a Facebook page or Twitter account. It's not that simple, as there are right and wrong strategies to use with each channel. Looking at these channels and their tactics, you'll learn how to develop, implement and measure social media activity.

Community & Customer Relationship Management

- Do you need help improving the efficiency and effectiveness of your marketing management?
- Do you have sufficient time and resources to create and distribute resources to your industry and customer base?
- Are your outreach efforts stagnant or causing disruptions to operations?
- Do you have a potential conflict of interest by handling your ongoing marketing programs with operational resources?

Global Help Desk & Support

- Do you support customers globally, but lack in-house bandwidth and expertise?
- Do you struggle to quantify the value of your marketing program?
- Are you tired of getting blamed for missed opportunities or slow response times?
- Do you have trouble tracking, prioritizing and resolving requests for support?

Marketing Automation Enablement

- Having trouble identifying or selecting marketing automation solutions?
- Do you want more out of your current go-to-market solution?
- Are you in need of consistent communication with your customers?
- Do you lack the budget for technology, but wish you could leverage technology without a capital investment?

Pre-Post M&A Support: Marketing Bridge

- Are you involved in the pre-acquisition due diligence process and concerned with successor liability?
- Do you lack bandwidth or expertise to integrate, oversee or transition a newly acquired company into your marketing program?
- Are you struggling to address customer acquisition risks identified during due diligence?

Agency of Record

- Do you want to grow your marketing team, but lack the budget?
- Do you wish you could leverage the best in industry digital marketing talent without sacrificing equity?
- Are you looking to create a narrative for potential business expansion?
- Do you want access to modular marketing growth without committing to multi-year contracts?

Opportunity Identification & Innovation Management

- Do you need help analyzing the potential savings and benefits from potential customer or product line expansion?
- Do you wish you had time to qualify marketing tools or implement a baseline for business growth?
- Do you have a go-to-marketing plan in place, but lack the staff to manage your day-to-day?

Third Party Vendor Management

- Do you lack the time or resources to audit and ensure your marketing vendors' quality and service performance level?
- Are you tired of correcting errors or performing your vendors' responsibilities?
- Are you unknowingly putting your Company's reputation and compliance at risk by relying on incorrect best practices and roadmap?
- When was the last time you audited your vendor's fees or timeliness of deliveries?

Marketing Program Optimization

- When was the last time you assessed your Company's marketing-related risks, gaps, and challenges?
- Do your processes and procedures reflect your current business requirements and risk tolerance?
- Is your staff configured to support a major marketing migration

www.ingramcontent.com/pod-product-compliance
Lightning Source LLC
Chambersburg PA
CBHW030542220526
45463CB00007B/2947